MW01093778

A BOOK OF ALCHEMY

BOOK OF THE CHEMICAL ART

First Edition 1518

Marsilius Ficinus

New Edition 2018

Edited by Tarl Warwick

A Book of Alchemy

COPYRIGHT AND DISCLAIMER

FOREWORD

This work, originally entitled *Liber de Arte Chemica* and originally produced in the 1500s by Marsilius Ficinus, delves into the more philosophical and, dare I say, skeptical side of alchemy. Possibly misattributed to Ficinus, and originating with some other Renaissance-era philosopher, it contains not only short passages on the generation of gold along with its alchemical predecessors (mercury and sulfur predominantly) but also fairly lengthy expositions on the evils of superstitious occult practice, seen as departed from the early scientific principle of alchemy itself.

Indeed, this same work contains as well, at its end, a detailed set of revelations regarding alchemical science supposedly delivered by the Devil to a necromancer- with the rest of the work primarily focused on the philosophical concept of likeness and the order of natural law, it seems that this short latter segment probably contains a hidden purpose; namely that it is ascribed wrongfully to necromancy, possibly to confuse laypeople into thinking the text is blasphemous (so they will be disinclined to think too deeply into its content), or perhaps to increase its circulation at the time it was printed.

As with many alchemical works the basic principle of the male and female generative force is likened to the actions of alchemical sulfur and mercury upon one another, through which the stone of the philosophers is said to be made. Unlike most such texts, though, here it is given a far more directly christianized and divine quality, with even the Virgin Mary herself likened to parts of the action of alchemical art. Within these pages there is not simply Catholic infusion, with allusions to various saints and to the same virgin, but also a small amount of what can only be said to be gnostic influence in addition to the same.

Likewise, here the similitude to nature is given; for the philosopher, it is said, is merely imitating nature, that same nature being given its divine order, by which the metals and other materials are purified. In the case of nature it takes place within the Earth, through the influence of vapor, and over a great length of time. By recreating these same speculative conditions the philosopher hopes to create such materials with greater speed by imitating the same natural forces. The basic concept of the generation of gold is, amusingly, essentially true- for seismic and volcanic forces (forces acting within the Earth, and within the same situation which gives rise to the upheaval of mountains) do indeed, over time, give rise to seams of gold in areas more easily extracted by man. Indeed, allusions to these forces may also be an example of a dual, hidden meaning.

It should be noted that this work is more theoretical and explanatory than it is hands-on.

A Book of Alchemy

Chapter I

Of the Generation of Metals in the Bowels of the Earth

The opinion and determination of all who believe rightly is the same: that all metals are generated by the vapor of sulfur, and of *argent vive*. because when the fat of the earth being heated, finds the substance of water somewhat congealed, it as well by its natural virtue, as by the rays of the celestial bodies and the endeavor of heaven, as according to the purity or impurity of each, consolidated it in the veins of the earth into those most beautiful bodies, gold, silver, copper, tin, iron, and lead.

Chapter II

Of Nature and Art

But there are in the arch of this world, two efficient causes, nature and art. Nature daily produces and generates new things. But art, by conception, making an impression of the similarity of those things upon herself, does in an admirable manner follow in the footsteps and designs of nature. So that if the wit of man does not sometime assist in some things, it is evident that nature herself had gone astray from her operation. Or art sometimes does by the help of nature, correct, supply and in a manner (especially in this magnificent discourse of mineral things) seems to exceed nature. Which has already been long since consecrated to perpetual memory by those ancient philosophers.

There are two sorts of philosophers. Some only searching into nature by herself, have in the mass of their writings delivered the virtue and power which sub-lunary things have, as well from the elemental qualities, as from heaven and the stars; as the physicians are. And some others who have described the natures of animals, trees, herbs, metals, and precious stones. But others truly are more glorious, penetrating most sagaciously and sharply not only into nature, but finally into the manner itself of nature, and into her more inward recesses, have by a truer title assumed to themselves the name of philosopher. But because nature produces all metals out of two things, sulfur and mercury, and has left us the superior bodies generated out of them, with the inferior bodies, certain is it is that the industrious may make the same out of her three operations, and reduce the inferior bodies to the nature and perfection of the superior bodies.

Chapter III

Refutes an Opinion of some in this Art, and the Philosophical Art is laid down in a very few words.

And because by most of the studious in philosophy it is granted that metals themselves are generated of sulfur and mercury, some have judged that sulfur and mercury, since they are the root and matter of metals, ought to be taken and so long purified, until they were combined together into a metallic body. These truly had they descended deeper into nature's sanctuary, would never have come to such foolish opinions. For though sulfur and mercury were as it were the root of metals before the first coagulation, yet now they are not, since they are brought to another nature: whence it remains that there cannot be made out of them any metallic body. Since also the chain is unknown, by which Venus and Mercury copulated together in due proportion.

Wherefore they are not to be taken, but rather that which is out of them fully purified in the womb of the earth, and that truly the most pure; whose like you will not find in a vegetable nature.

It is evident that all little trees, flowers and small herbs are produced from water and the union of a subtle earth. And if you endeavor to produce a tree or an herb, you must not take earth or water, but rather that which is from them, as a scion or a seed, which being committed to the bosom of the earth, the parent of all things, and cherished with a nutriment of their own nature, and called forth by the darting of the solar light, do in due time break out into the surface of the earth, into the species of a tree or an herb. In like manner that divine art teaches how to take the seed our of the more perfect body; which being put into the philosophical earth prepared by art and continually purified by a temperate heat into a white or red powder, is said to have converted the inferior bodies into the nature of the superior.

Chapter IV

Speaks of why the Philosophers have sought for this Art, but found it not, and this Question is resolved: why the Spirit in Metals cannot Propagate its like, since the Spirit of everything is the Author of Generation.

But we readily affirm that the inspiration of God was the chief cause why those ancient philosophers searched after this science. For the philosophers seeing that all vegetable and animal things, as also other things, do by a certain spirit of their own multiply themselves, and that a transmutation is in this inferior world made by the air, which seemed in a long time to corrupt all particular things, and that their nature changed itself by the motions of another thing: There arose among them this question, namely, why the spirit in metals could not propagate its like, since out of one scion there grew many, and out of one little grain almost innumerable grains did multiply themselves. It was at length decreed by the divine oracle, that the spirit was withheld by a grosser matter, which spirit if it were separated by a certain sublimation at the fires and being separated were preserved in its own proper place, it might as a seminal virtue, without any untruth, generate its like. From hence the philosophers thought to bring the light and luster of the most perfect body into the inferior bodies since they had found that they differed among themselves only according to the purification method, either greater or less, and the mercury was the first original of all metals, with which mercury extracting the metallic part of gold, they brought gold to the first nature. Which reduction indeed since it is easy and possible, it was by the philosophers concluded that a transmutation in metals is easy and possible. And when these primitive philosophers had reduced gold into the first matter, they made use of the celestial influence, that it might not be made a metal again such as it was before. Afterward they purified its nature, separating the unclean from the clean. Which being done they called that thing, the transmuting stone of the philosophers. For the making whereof several operations have been invented by several philosophers, that that might be completed by art which was left by nature; since nature herself is always inclined toward her own perfection.

Chapter V

Treats of What the Philosophers' Stone is, and Discourses first of its First Part.

And because the philosophers had so obscurely set forth this science in strange involvement of words and shadows of figures, the stone of the philosophers was doubted by a very many men. It was asked, of what things is it made? But if you will mind diligently, we divide the stone into two parts. The first part we say is terrestrial Sol, wherein both the ancient philosophers and the more modern do plainly agree with me in their testimonies in the Turba. Without terrestrial Sol the physical work is not perfected.

Since they all assert that there is no true tincture without their *Aqua Regia* brass because in that there is the most pure sulfur of the wise, in which sagacious nature contains her seed. And as the sun diffuses and darts down most lively and penetrating rays on this elementary world. So the stone of the philosophers being by a physical operation made out of gold, the son, as I may say, of the sun, disperses itself into other metals, and will forever equalize them to himself in virtue, color, and weight. And because of all metals, we deservedly take gold before all others. For since we would make gold and silver, it is necessary to take the same. Man is generated out of man, a tree from a tree, and herb produces an herb, and a lion a lion; since each thing according to the temper of its nature, which they call the completion, generates and produces its like. Yet the philosophers more truly do not make gold or silver, but nature cleansed by the skill of the operator.

Chapter VI

Treats of the Second Part of the Stone, Where the Spirit is Compared to the most Glorious Virgin Saint Mary.

We say the *argent vive* is the second part of the stone. Which since it is living and crude, is said to dissolve the bodies themselves, because it naturally adheres to them in their

9

profundity. This is the stone without which nature operates nothing. Whence the philosophers advise us not to work but in Sol and mercury; which being joined make up the stone of the philosophers. Who therefore can deservedly praise the merits of mercury, since it is he alone who makes gold thin and who has so great a power, that he can reduce Sol itself into the first nature? Which power nothing else in the world is discerned to have. It is thus said of the mercury which the wise men seek that is in mercury. Mercury destroys all foliated Sol: it dissolves and softens it, and takes the soul out of the body. If it be sublimated, then there is made *aqua vitae*. If anyone therefore should ask you: What are the stones? You shall answer, that Sol and mercury are the physical stones. But these stones are dead on Earth and operate nothing, but what is by the industry of men supplied to them.

I will propose you a similitude of gold. The ethereal heaven was shut from all men, so that all men should descend to the infernal seats, and be there perpetually detained. But Jesus Christ opened the gate of the ethereal Olympus, and has now unlocked the kingdoms of Pluto, that the souls may be taken out; when by the cooperation of the holy spirit in the virginal womb, the Virgin Mary did by an ineffable mystery and most profound sacraments conceive what was the most excellent in the heavens and on the earth; and at length brought forth for us the savior of the whole world, who out of his super abundant bounty shall save all who are able to sin, if the sinner turn himself to him. But she remained an untouched and undefiled virgin: whence mercury is not undeservedly compared to the most glorious saint the Virgin Mary. For mercury is a virgin because it never propagated in the womb of the Earth and metallic body, and yet it generates the stone for us; by dissolving heaven, that is, gold, it opens it, and brings out the soul; which understand you to be the divinity, and carries it some little while in its womb, and at length in its own time transmits it into a cleansed body. From whence a child, that is, the stone, is born to us, by whose blood the inferior bodies being tinged are brought safe into the golden heaven, and mercury remains a virgin without a stain, such as is was ever before.

Chapter VII

Determines why the Philosophers have hidden this Knowledge: where the Praise of the Art is set down, and He Inveighs against Zoilus the Carper as the Philosophers.

But Hamul in *Senior* declares the chief cause why the philosophers have delivered this art down to posterity and the sons of wisdom, by uncertain similitude and obscure allegories: that they might attribute it to the glorious God who might reveal it to whom he would, and prohibit it from whom he would. Rasis also in the book, 'The Light of Lights', reports: "For if I should explain all things according to what they are, there would be no further occasion of prudence, but the fool would be made equal to the wise man." We read also in the end of the Turba: "For unless the names were multiplied in this physical art, children would deride our knowledge. Wherefore we do not much value those who object ignorantly to our divine art as adulterate; from which the most famous philosophers used to take all the knowledge of almost all things; as heretofore the statuaries did the thefts and the threads of our art, from the statue of Polycletus. It would also be most absurd to suspect that those ancient philosophers of venerable authority, especially in this discourse of natural things, have delivered down anything of falsehood to posterity, who employed their chiefest labor in inquiring after truth, although they ascended not to the sublimeness of the saving nature of faith, and the greatest height of the divine essence." Who, therefore, but Zoilus, would not praise this science, and particularly favor it? From whence almost all the arts of these detractors are taken: from which so many colors very useful for the art of picture drawing derive their beginning. I say nothing of the art of money making: I pass by the learned distillation of the physicians, whereby they use to draw out the virtue, which they call a quintessence. Which shall I say of those brazen vessels wherewith we make lightening and thunder among men? If they did but use them only against the sacrilegious enemies of the christian faith.

Besides the science of the stone is so sublime and magnificent, that therein almost all nature and the whole universe of beings is beheld, as in a certain clear looking glass. For it is like a lesser world, where there are the four elements, and a fifth essence, which they call heaven in which another most noble essence has placed its seat, which some philosophers have used to compare (with reverence it should be spoken) to the omnipotent God, and the most holy and undivided Trinity, which is neither of the nature of the heaven, nor of the natures of the elements: and they have called it by a particular name, the soul, the middle nature. And as God the maker of the world: so this essence, which is called by the title of a God, is everywhere in the whole world, it is, in the physical glass. And as the omnipotent God is immense in the procreation of its like, even to the last end of the greater world. For then the generative nature shall be taken away from every procreating thing. From which words one skillful in nature may gather, that the stone can tinge many parts; whereby also many other difficulties may be removed. Then out upon Aristarchus who blushes not to profess himself an interpreter of the divine writings, and yet fears not with his most impudent railing to attack this knowledge of a nature created by God; than which, next after the sacred writings, God has conferred on this world nothing more magnificent and more sublime.

A Book of Alchemy

Tell me by the immortal God, what is more unjust than for men to hate what they are ignorant of? And then if the thing do deserve hatred, what is of all things more shallow? What more abject? Or what greater madness and stupidity is there, than to condemn that science in which you have concerned yourself just nothing at? Who has never learned either nature or the majesty of nature, or the property or the occult operations of metals. The counselor also babbles and croaks, and the misusers of the law, the greatest haters of philosophy, who with the hammer of a venal tongue coin themselves money out of the tears of the miserable: who shipping over the most sacred of laws, have by the intricacies of their expositions persecuted all the world with their frauds. But why do I go after jeers and satyrs? Let these crabbed fellows and their followers remain perpetually in their opinion, they who know nothing. Which is honest, which is pleasant, which is delightful, which lastly is anything elevated above a vulgar doctrine: and who have attained at nothing glorious and famous, but perhaps at some plebeian business from the black sons of Cadamus. But to which purpose are these? I have made the choice of this stone of the philosophers familiar to me; and I very often call it the only Minerva, and the greatest pearl of all occult philosophy, or of magic, not indeed of the superstitious, but of the natural. Yet it seems in the opinion of the unlearned to degenerate far from a better study: which is decreed and ordained by the divine will.

Chapter VIII

Treats of the first Essence of all things: and it is here discussed what Nature is, what the soul the middle nature, what the soul of the world, where that very great error is confuted of philosophers asserting the world to be an animal, and it is disputed that there is only a human soul; by a participation or likeness of which, there seems to be a brutal soul. And that the sun is the eye of the world and the heart of heaven.

I have now a mind, candid reader, to procure you something concerning the secrets of nature, both out of philosophical, and the theological corpus. Since I have perceived that many of the ancients as also of the more modern have taken great pains in searching after nature, nobody but one beside himself will deny that those things will be of use to the whole academy and exercise of philosophy. But here the cradle of nature is to be looked for a higher, do not therefore think it pious, if I make a digression a little further than perhaps this undertaking may require.

The most glorious God, the contriver, and the ineffable author of all things, before the beginning of the world, wanting nothing, but all-sufficient to himself, and forever remaining in the most profound retirement of his divinity, being out of his most abundant beauty willing, that the things from all eternity foreknown should proceed into existence, created in the beginning a certain essence of them, in rough draughts, as I may say, as yet unformed, which Moses, he whom I am to stile the fountain and chief president of the philosophy of the philosophers, does sometimes call a void and empty earth, sometimes an abyss and water, but Anaxagoras a confused chaos. Others have rightly termed it, the mother of the world, the foundation and the face of nature. Within whose womb when all things lay undistinguished and undigested, nor more conspicuous in their proper forms, the artificial creator, did by the intervening spirit of God exactly and regularly drawn and describe this visible world, according to copy and the similitude of the intelligible world. Hence he with shining fires most workman-like adorned the heavens hung up on high, and so ordered and designed the motion of them, and of the stars, that they should in a wonderful manner run about the arch of heaven, for the formation of the varieties of the seasons succeeding one another; and that by their motion and light they might warm, cherish and preserve in their beings the inferior things. Therefore he laid the inferior things beneath the superior, as an egg to be hatched under a hen, or as a woman to be made fruitful by a man. Into which he from the beginning inserted certain seminal reasons, that they might, taking their opportunities, multiply themselves, as I may say, with a perpetual fertility and offspring. But God wrought out his compacted being of the world by certain harmony and musical proportion allayed to one another, that which are in the superior world are in the inferior also, but in a terrestrial manner: that which likeness are in the inferiors, may also be seen in the superior, in a celestial manner indeed, and according to the cause.

To which you may perhaps apply the opinion of Anaxagoras, holding that everything is in everything. Wherefore it is agreeable that God should rule and fill up all which he created. Nor do we therefore say that God does fill up all things, that they should contain him, but that they rather should be contained by him. Neither is it to be thought that God is in all things so that each thing according to the proportion of its size may contain him, that is the greater things the more, and the

lesser the less. But God so fills up all things that there is not
anything where he is not. And we therefore understand within all
things, but not included without all things, but not excluded: and
therefore to be the interior, that by his incomprehensible
magnitude he may include all things. Therefore Saint Dennis
says: "That all things may be affirmed of God, since he is the
author and governor." On the contrary, that all things are more
truly denied of him, since he is nothing of those things which he
created. Which seems to me more acceptable and more certain,
as well by the variable course of this world, as for the
unsearchable abyss of his most exalted divinity. For God has
placed the greatest distance between him and the created things.
But God is truly immense and ineffable, not to be discovered, not
to be understood, above all imagination, above all thought, above
all understanding, above all essence, unnameable, to be by
silence alone proclaimed in the heart: the most powerful, the
most wise, the most clement: the father, the world, the holy
spirit; and altitude incomprehensible, a trinity indivisible, an
essence immutable. Whose image is all nature, though the eye
never be so intent. Who is the unity of all creatures, and main
point, and the only one; who is stronger than all power, greater
than all excellence, better than all praise. Whom the divine Plato
made to inhabit in a fiery substance, meaning, that is, the
ineffable splendor of God in himself, and love around himself.
Whom others have asserted to be an intellectual and fiery spirit,
having no form but transforming itself into so ever it would and
co-equalizing to all things universally. Who in a manifold way is
as it were joined to his creatures. Again going forth from that his
infinity eternity and omnipotence, he by a fervent love, sincere
faith and solid hope may be placed in the purified minds of men.
Let whom be blessed for all thousands of thousands of ages.

   We said a little before that God was unnameable, whom
Martinus Capella says that *Arithmetica* saluted by a proper name,

when going to salute Jove, she with her fingers folded down into them, made up seven hundred, ten and seven numbers. But what that most noble number means, and its division into its members, the Arithmetician knows; not he who inquires into the mercantile way of numbering but into proportions. In this number we discover all numbers, and every proportion both musical and geometrical. Add something of greater moment. That in these numbers the name of God is most exactly found. Whose most holy and forever adorable name is in this fullness of time set down in five letters. When in the time of nature it was written with three, and of the law with four. We say moreover that God has every name, because all things are in him, and he is in all things: as shall hereafter be disputed of, and yet has no name, because a fitting name cannot be given to the divine majesty. But how much mystery and strength numbering has in itself, I easily believe the Pythagoreans knew very well, who called one number Pallas, another Diana, another the father, another the mother, and finally one the male, and another the female: and those who had the greatest knowledge in the numeral science, applied the monas thereby united to God the creator: But the dias or duality to matter: to forms themselves the virgin trias or three: then to man and to his life hexas and heptas the six and seven. But the eneas or ten they not a miss, and did very handsomely apply to all creatures.

But to return to the purpose, hear Dionysius repeating: That God is in all things, or all things are in God, as numbers are in unity, as in the center of the circle are all the right lines: and as the soul is the strength of the members. Because as the unity is the common measure, fountain and original of all numbers, and containing in itself every number entirely conjoined, is the beginning of all multitude. But guiltless of all multitudes is always the same and immutable; so in like manner are created things toward the creator. And as an individual soul, is the ruler of its body, and the whole present to the whole body, and to every part of it: so God is everywhere in this world and fills and governs, and perpetually preserves it by the virtue which he daily infuses liberally into created things out of the eternal fountain of his spirit. From whence we rightly by a certain similitude of the soul, do call the God of nature or the power of God, by which he maintains all things, a soul, a middle nature, or the soul of the world. Not that the world itself is an animal, which we may explode from the entrance into christian philosophy, partly the christian metaphysics, and partly in this consideration of the stone.

But the sublime state of the nature hereof requires to be composed in a loftier style; we have here chosen a lower sort of speech; and we place the soul of the world chiefly in the sun. For there is nothing in the soul of the firmament, beside a soul, which represents a greater similitude of God than light itself. Since everything does challenge to itself so much of God, as I may say, as they are capable of light. And since nothing is more conspicuous bright-eyed than the sun, many of the Platonists chiefly imitating Orpheus herein have termed the sun, the eye of the world. Because all things were seen and shown themselves in it as in a certain most bright mirror. Hence Heraclitus says, that all things would perish, should you take the sun out of the world. What is this small body of ours, if the soul be away? No vein having a pulse is to be felt there, there is in it no show of sense, no vital breath nor any respiration therein. Wherefore it also seemed good to some to call the sun the heart of heaven. Because as in the heart there is the only fountain of blood moistening and reddening the other members of the human body, and infusing a vital motion: So there seems to be in the sun the vegetation and preservation of all, as well inferior as well as superior things. Because he by this light inspires as it were, life and heat into inferior things. But light is a certain simple of single action converting all things unto itself by an enlivening warmth, passing through all beings, carrying their virtues and qualities through all and dispersing darkness and obscurity. Phoebus therefore resides in the middle with his refulgent locks, as king and emperor of the world, holding a scepter of the government: in whom that there is all the virtue of the celestials, nor only Iamblichus, but many others have confirmed. And also Proclus says: "At the sun's aspect, that all the powers of all celestial things are gathered together and collected into one, which we believe are gathered together and collected into one, which we believe are at length through his fiery breathing have spread over this lower world." This also may be even a mighty argument to you: that the sun approaching toward us, the earth grows full of herbs and ripens, but when he departs it withers. But I now delight to make some comment on the infancy of nature.

Chapter IX

Of Nature.

We affirm nature to be a certain power implanted in things producing like things out of like. For nature generates, augments and nourishes all things. Wherefore it has in itself the names of all things. An animal is from nature; a stone, wood, a tree, and the bodies which you see are from nature and her maintaining. Nature is the blood of the elements, and the power of mixing which brings to pass the mixtures of the elements in everything in this sub-lunary world, and has imprinted on them a form agreeable to their species, by which that thing is distinguishable and separated from each other thing. Nor is nature of any color, yet a partaker and efficient of all colors: also of no weight, nor quality, but finally the fruitful parent of all qualities and things. What is therefore nature? God is nature, and nature is God: understand it thus- out of God there arises something next to him.

Nature is therefore a certain invisible fire, by which Zoroaster taught that all things were begotten, to whom Heraclitus the Ephesian seems to give consent. Did not the spirit of the Lord, which is a fiery love, when it was carried on the waters, put into them a certain fiery vigor? Since nothing can be generated without heat. God inspired into created things, when it was said in the generation of the world; increase and be multiplied, a certain germination, that is, a greenness, by which all things might multiply themselves. Whence some more profoundly speculative, said that all things were green, is called to grow and increase, and that greenness they named nature. But Aristotle says: That motion being unknown, nature is unknown, since it is now volatile and in a continual motion of generation, augmentation and alteration, which at length in the latter end of the world, shall be stable and fixed. Because God will then take away from things that virtue and power of generating, and will place it in the most inward treasure of his omnipotence, where it was from eternity. I therefore had a mind to call this virtue of generation and of the preservation of things, the soul of the world. Not that the world is an animal, as the Platonic accounts and the testimonies of the Arabian, Egyptian, and Chaldean astrologers seem to approve. For the philosophers maintained the world to be an animal, and the heavens and the stars to be animals, and the souls of things to be intelligent, participating of the divine mind. Moreover that a God or certain soul presided over everything and that all things were full of Gods, was the opinion of Democritus and Orpheus and of many of the Pythagoreans: to whom they ordained divine honors. And to the same they dedicated prayers and sacrifices and revered them with diverse sorts of worship. Besides they reduced all such souls into one soul of the world. They likewise referred all their

A Book of Alchemy

Gods unto one Jove. This Aristotle and the Aristotelian
Theophrastus, this Avicenna, Algozeles; this the Stoics and all
the Peripatetics do confess, and with their utmost power have
endeavored to prove. I do not doubt but that from hence sprung
all the error of gentility: from hence the fictions of the poets, the
diabolical sacrifices and sacrilegious victims. Hence the
Egyptian land did in their chapels worship and adore some
certain animals and other prodigious monsters. Who will not say
therefore that the philosophy of the heathens is vain? Which was
most miserably ruined by this common error, and by many
others: where the philosophers seemed to me to be most like the
beehives, or children busying themselves with bottomless vessels
to drain a great well.

      Yet we may think them worthy of forgiveness since there
had not shined to them the true light, Jesus Christ the savior.
Therefore it behooves the Christian philosopher whose authority
is graver, and judgment more certain to bring within the verge of
the Catholic Church, which things so ever seem to make for the
obligation of the nature of the faith as being possessed by unjust
heirs: after the manner of Virgil who said he gathered Gold out
of the dunghill of Ennius. Also like little bees, while they suck
out the sweetest among the flowers of Hymettus and Hybla for
the sake of making honey. Who is there who would not bewail
with tears, the untimely death of Picus of Mirandolla, whom the
fatal sisters have particularly envied to our Age. Who had he
little longer enjoyed life; would have trimmed up with new
beauty, the tattered and begging philosophy, blotting out all of its
errors. Yet let everyone highly praise the lawful philosophy,
whose foundation is nature, or the world, and which prescribes
manners and virtue to man. Which does correct for you the first
youthful years and rudiments of your life. Which challenges to
itself the interpretation of nature, and the search of things the
most abstruse from our eyes. Most worthily true to which the

scanning of divine and human things should be referred. We thereby as much as we can by the divine favor and by natural light inquiry into the recesses of the world, into the earth and the tracts of the seas, and the high heavens. This describes heaven and the immeasurable multitude of stars, as also the journey of the golden haired sun, and the laborious eclipses of the moon. This, with a geometrical staff, describes the ways of the stars.

This teaches the Aeolian bellows and whispers of the winds, which Hippotades does with his scepter rule.
Why the mass of the earth does stagger, what makes the rainbow's arch, and hoary snows and frigid frosts. What breeds the dew, the lightning, what the hollow fleeces of the clouds, the swellings of the Earth, and the three forked thunderbolt.

What gathers showers, what the shining hail; what are the seeds of gold, what of Iron; whence cruel thunder, whence the fountains of continual waters take their beginning, and such like other things. Let tender youths in their childhood learn that philosophy; and everywhere avoid the doting fables of those philosophers who hold the world to be animal, and that it consists of innumerable animals, and those divine. What is more vain, what is more idle? For what else is it to say, the sun is animated, or the celestial bodies are animated, and participating of the divine mind, than to fall into an evil heresy, and the abominable falsehood of idolatry? Neither is it to be granted (witness Saint Augustine) that those sidereal globes do live by certain minds of their own, and those intellectual and blessed. I do certainly know that only a human soul is divine light, created according to the image of the word, the cause of causes, and the first pattern; marks with the substance of the seal of God: and whose impression is the eternal word. By a participation of which we believe the brutal soul to subsist, taken out of the bosom of nature, seeming to have a slender similitude and small footstep of a rational soul, as the echo is the image and resemblance of a living voice. But let others look after the vegetable soul.

The theological doctors admit intelligence moves of the orbs; not that they inform the orbs themselves, or (according to the opinion of Saint Jerome) make them intellectual and sensible, but to assist them in moving.

Though also those orbs might (the divine will so commanding) be voluble of their own accord. Yet the omnipotent God out of his ineffable bounty, would have second causes to preside over this worldly fabric, that whosoever does move themselves, does also give to others the power of moving. Whence also he also deputed angels for the custody of human souls, though he also primarily guarded himself. Yet it is not to be thought that such like intelligences are necessarily applied to turn the spheres, as if they could not be turned about by their own rotation; when some busy men do in like manner frame that heavenly machine of copper or brass, fixing the earth in the very middle. Then they afterwards with certain little wheels affix the other elements, also the orbs of the stars and heavens, whereby they endeavor exactly to express the motion of the planets and the face of heaven. There are other curious men who endeavor to frame clocks and also certain mills which should turn perpetually. If man can imitate the divine method, who would not believe that those sidereal globes by their own power may be wheeled about?

But what shall I say of the vain astrology, which our Picus of Mirandolla, famed in all sorts of learning, has sometime since by forcible reasons overthrown? Tell me, why astrologer, why refer you all things to heaven? Why do you romance about the natures of the stars and the signs, and of the motions of the planets? Who can by no means guess at the force and property of even the least terrestrial thing? Why should you fear the constellations and the stars, or rather lie? Who cannot by dimensions comprehend any little earthen body. What is more ridiculous, what more absurd, that have not in the ninth or tenth heaven to catch at such configurations and images of lines, or at the figures of the eighth heaven from the wandering application of the stars? What power do you think such imagined images have? What do the triplicities, what do the aspects of those stars and the rest of such like books void of the truth and virtue pretend to? Although such motions and the natures of the stars, and various applications of things to one another should seem to have some signification, yet I am persuaded man cannot well know them unless it were shown to them by some miracle from heaven. Hence Saint Jerome thus derides astrologers and nativity calculators. These are they who lift up themselves against God's knowledge and all which is acted in the world, promising themselves a fictitious science, they refer to rising and setting of stars. These are they who are vulgarly called mathematicians, and think human affairs to be governed by the course and ways of the stars: and when they promise safety to others, know not their own punishments. I, while I was yet in the city Agrippa played thus upon the astrologer. In my opinion it commonly happens to those astrologers, as it did to Thales Milesius heretofore, who when he went out of his house to gaze at the stars, is said to have fallen into a ditch underneath him. Who when he ridiculed an old woman, being laughed at by her, he returned home with shame. Wherefore, oh Christian philosopher, send away into perpetual banishment beyond the Caspian mountains, such like foolish chattering of astrology, and its daughters geomancy, hydromancy, pyromancy, necromancy, soothsaying, and many other such charades with what other vulgarly resembles them and do not attribute to his creatures the glory of the omnipotent Lord God. Now let us see what nature the philosophers inquired after.

Chapter X

What the Philosophers, and what sort of Nature they would have: where the spirit is said to be the ethereal chariot of the soul.

The stone which the philosophers do seek is an invisible and impalpable spirit; it is a tincture and a tinging spirit: which indeed another visible and palpable spirit has hidden in its innermost bowels. Even so the philosophers have left us the same spirit undiscovered, under the veil of enigmas that the stone is a fifth separated from four. It is the bond of the elements, the medium and the chain, which has made the elements of God agree, and which in the womb of the earth combined sulfur and mercury into a metallic body. And because such a bond, as is in the earth, since it is invisible cannot be had, the philosophers sought after it in the more perfect body. The philosophers do therefore inquire after the generative nature, which may be able to generate metals, that they cleanse it, and make it a hundred thousand times more potent in tincture than it was at first in nature. And they accustomed themselves to call it a living fire, or the living fire of nature, or by a secret word, the soul of the middle nature. And as physicians distinguish man into body, spirit, and soul, in like manner the philosophers have divided the stone into those parts.

Sometimes the spirit is the life of the soul, the soul is the life of the spirit. Again those two are the life of the body. The spirit is also the tie of the soul and the body, and as it were the ethereal chariot or vehicle of the soul, which spreads abroad the virtue of the soul through the whole body. You may also understand the four elements, when the philosophers affirm that the stone consists of body, spirit, and soul. For the water is spirit; also air: the middle fire, as I may say, is spirit. The earth we call not spirit but body, because it is the retainer, the matter and the seat of the other elements.

Chapter XI

Teaches that Solution is Necessary, by which the generative spirit is brought out of the body.

But such a tie cannot be easily had, by reason of the most strong compaction of gold itself, except by solution, which is the foundation and beginning of this noble science, in which the arcanum of all nature does consist. It is the treasure of this affair. It is that which lifts up the poor man from the dunghill and equals him to kings and princes. Whence the philosophers demand why the bodies, that is, gold and silver are dissolved. They answer: That the pure may be separated from the impure. For the body is for this reason dissolved, that the earth itself may be cleansed in the profundity. Which nature could not, because she operates simply. And in that cleansing the impediments of the tincture is away, so that it may innumerably propagate its like. But if so be that this propagation of its like be made by the spirit, since every spirit is the author of generation, and it is hindered by grosser matter, we say that solution is necessary, by which gold may be made living, and as I may say, spiritual, and be reduced into the first nature, that is into the spirit of the water, and the vapor of the earth, that there may at length be had such a sulfur and a mercury with us, out of which metals are generated, in the womb of the earth. But solution is perfected when you shall have separated the soul and the spirit of gold. But because with philosophers gold is the most temperate body, having equal parts of hot, cold, moist and dry. Therefore it may with the more difficulty be corrupted and dissolved by reason of the equal agreement and proportion of the elements. Therefore there must a disagreement be made among the elements by contrary elements: and this discord makes a solution and mortification of the body: which being done there is made a cleansing humidification of nature, which nevertheless cannot be done without a physical separation of the elements. But the elements of the body must be so separated, that the generative nature may remain in its flower and bud. That if anyone should burn that flower, and separate the elements from one another, the generative sperm would be lost; nor would any creature be able to join them anymore, so as they should generate. This is the truest consideration of the philosophers. If any out of his own fancy consider otherwise, he is indeed a natural fool, and makes syllogisms against nature.

Chapter XII

Disputes of Hidden Things in the Art, and about threefold separation.

But you sons of wisdom, there are three solutions in the physical work. The first is of the crude body, the second is of the physical earth, the third we place in the augmentation. There are also in the solution these three hidden things: the weight, the measure of time, and fire. Wherefore if you know the weight of mercury and gold, and the measure of time, how long solution is in the making, and in a temperate fire, you have solution: which ought to be made in the secret furnace, and a little larger glasses. Wherefore diverse fires are to be procured, and so different parts to be put in glasses; that you may at last endowed with divine favor, find it out. You must also distinguish in this admirable work the days, months and years of the philosophers. The philosophers affirm, that if you, you may make the trial in three natural days. That if you are of a sprightlier wit, say they, you may distinguish it in twenty four hours. They in philosophy have appointed two nights and three days. Beseech the greatest and highest God that you may be worthy to the last red day. The philosophers also lay down three keys, solution, conjunction, and fixation. Or if you profoundly understand them, three separations. First there is made the separation of the soul from the body by the spirit. Secondly the grimes themselves, which have shown themselves in the solution, are separated from the soul and spirit. Lastly the spirit shall be separated from the soul and this happens in the fixation of nature: so that hereafter and here I shall have told you so great secrets, that it cannot be believed. I do faithfully affirm two keys in the whole circle of philosophy. The first indeed which opens the body may be distributed into several keys. For what thing soever shall dissolve gold and reduce it into a spirit is called a key, though only one among others be the most powerful and natural key, as I wrote in chapter eight. And such a thing is called the stone. The second key which shuts up and does retain and coagulate the tinging spirit, we term the earth alone, which all philosophers have called the principle stone. But of the crow's head we freely profess, that all the philosophers from the beginning of the world have had so little, that it can hardly be believed. Yet the miserable satirists have thought that blackness which appeared in the surfaces, out of the superfluity of the mercury and the body to be the crow's head.

Chapter XIII

Treats of the Praxis of the Stone, of its first solution, and separation: where the arcanum of Nature, otherwise most abstruse, is laid open to a son of wisdom, in which Lucifer falls out of heaven.

A Book of Alchemy

It is now time, oh son of wisdom, to turn my pen to the practical part, where I would first warn everyone given to philosophy, that all kinds of salts, alums, and of many other and of foreign things are in vain, and bring with them nothing moment or efficacy. Likewise that all common solutions and vulgar sublimation are adulterate works and belong nothing to the true and natural science of the philosophers. Wherefore I judge that those mountebanks are to be avoided who with their refinings and rubifications have cheated almost all the world, in whom there is no vein of philosophy, which is warm, and who are rather to be esteemed false philosophers, since nothing is dearer to philosophers than the truth, nothing more foul than falsehood and deceit. Whereby it comes to pass that there are fewer philosophers, than you have perhaps believed. Now let us descend to the praxis, which we will divide into two works. In the first mention shall be made of the first solution, and of separation and distillation. In the second we will treat of conjunction and fixation, where consideration will be had of the most secret augmentation, which you will find in no book in the world. But here I have a mind to bring in the degrees of all the work wholly. For first we compound, the compound we putrefy, the putrefied we dissolve, the dissolved we divide, the divided we cleanse, the cleansed we unite, and so the work is accomplished. But to speak of these, each particularly, shall be our labor. But the philosophers are of opinion that in the praxis of the stone less than a twelfth part of mercury aught to be taken. But there is also among them a trial of the dissolved body, if it be squeezed through a leather.

Some also of the more modern have thought, that solution may be made in a shorter time if a long pounding or grinding of the gold by itself were first made by a certain mill or in a mortar. First therefore let the copper be purified with common salt prepared or with any other fitting thing, that its most subtle substance may be had. Let some parts of this purified water be mixed very well with one part of the most fine gold, reduce into leaves or thin spangles, and let them be put in a long glass with a hollow belly, stopped with little pieces of cloth, and with the sign of the cross, and let the glass be covered with ashes, up to the surface of the water, and let a very gentle heat be given, that the matter may not seem to ascend, but remain live with the gold, and let that equally balanced heat be kept so long a while, until in the water of mercury there out upon it a certain vaporous and subtle earth, which in a wonderful color is wont to be known when it is to be extracted. But the sulfur itself shines like a rainbow through the waters, yet not with all colors, like the rainbow in this greater world. The arch is itself of the rainbow stands half in the pure liquid and fluent water, and half upon the earth. Hence the whole property of and its natural similitude is shown by the iris, the rainbow: nor is the rainbow seen in heaven, but when the sun shines, which also uses to be followed by rain. But mists or thick clouds coming on, the sun itself, and also the arch of the rainbow is hidden. It pleased the natural philosophers to thus explain the rainbow: when the sun colors a moist and hollow cloud, and is thick like a looking glass, and intersects the middle of its orb: which comes nearer to our divine and admirable science. Yet it is not to be thought that the sulfur itself grows black when you extract it, as some have thought. The copper being at length extracted, you shall distill the water, in which there is the soul of gold or the metallic mercury of gold, with a slow heat, so that three core minutes may be counted between drop and drop. And that distilled water is called, our living water, which enlivens all bodies, and is composed of two natures: understand spirit, soul, and ferment, because the spirit is the seat of the soul, and its retaining bond. And this water is called by many names, the most sharp vinegar, lunar water, the woman's sperm, or the feminine menstruate, heaven, mercury, the hair of the red man, that is, the spirit of Sol, that is of gold: But the sulfur is called the body, the male Sol, the male sperm, earth and mercury. But these distillations are necessary, by which mercury is purified from all terrestrial rot, and Lucifer, that is, the uncleanness and the accursed earth falls down out of the golden heaven, and here a separation is made of the grime from the soul, as I disputed in chapter twelve. Here is a lofty similitude: heaven, that is, gold was pure in the original but when it was dissolved it showed corruption. Therefore the fist evil was in heaven, while as yet there was corruption and Lucifer, after whose fall heaven was so cleansed that no angel can now fall down out of the golden heaven. But if so be that Lucifer had had within himself, a soul of a middle nature, or a God, he could by no means have been thrust down to the infernal.

Chapter XIV

Disputes about the Second Part of the Praxis, where there is a more secret dispute about the fire and the colors: and these questions are resolved: Whether heaven ought to descend to the earth: Or the earth ascend into heaven: Or whether both ought to remain beneath heaven? Where the spirit is compared to an angel, who seems to descend with a human soul into a body.

There now remains the second part of the physical praxis, the far harder indeed, and far more sublime. In which we read that all the nerves of wit, and at length all the races of the mind of many philosophers have languished. For you would with more difficulty make a man revive, than put him to death. Here the work of God is required. It is indeed the greatest mystery to create souls, and frame an inanimate body into a living statue. Do you not think it is the business of a sprightly Wit to reduce the soul to the spirit, then the spirit to the soul, then again those two to the body? In this body of ours, it is requisite to know, how much the spirit is, how much the soul, and how much the body. Furthermore how much of the soul the middle nature, is in the spirit, and how much in the body, that by this you may join as it were two natures of the same kind, and akin to one another in due proportion. We ought therefore to join two waters, the sulfur of gold, and the soul and body of its mercury, Sol and Lune, the male and female, two generative forces, heaven and earth, and two, as I may say, *Argent vives*, and out of which alone the philosophers say their stone is made; which pitiful fellows mistake for crude mercury. But that mercury is all metals, male and female, and an hermaphrodite creation in the very marriage of the soul and the body, which I call solution; and the putrefaction of the philosophers. The earth of gold is dissolved by its own spirit, which you shall discover in these proportions. The body must be dissolved in the subtlest middle air: The body is also dissolved by its own heat and humidity; where the soul, the middle nature holds the principality in the color of blackness all in the glass: which blackness of nature the ancient philosophers called the crows head, or the black sun.

From whence a certain person advanced this proposition. I saw three circles encompassing one another, three suns in the firmament having three faces, that is, a black, a white, and a red sun. That blackness was also called by the name of all black things; after which all the colors of the world, which can be conceived by wit, use to appear, which at length are brought to a true whiteness, as to a center and principle point. In white there are all colors, and from that the rest seem, as I may say, to be colored. White and black by nature herself are colors, and indeed the extremes, out of the manifold mixture and proportion of which with one another we believe the middle colors, as they are called, to arise. We hold also that from the confounding black and white together there is prepared a certain redness. But that whiteness we call the white stone, the white sun, the full moon, and calcined Lune, white silver, the white earth, fruitful, cleansed and calcined, the white Calx, and the salt of the metals, and the calcined body, and we call it by many other names. It is moreover called the living earth, and the living and white sulfur, when the soul has been reduced into the body, and the impediment removed. Here we resolve this question: Whether the earth ought to be airy or fiery? We say both at once. If so be it were only fiery, it would be burned into the ashes of the dead. But if only airy, being made volatile it would vanish away in tinging metals.

But what shall I say of the fire whereby the dissolution of the Earth is made? Behold the heat in the bowels of the earth, which nature alone supplies: where you seem as it were to perceive none; which being then excited by the sun's heat, does in the metal-breeding mountains by ascending and descending for many cubits coagulate everywhere the thicker water, and together with the fatness of the earth associates them into one body. But since nature does scarcely sometimes in five hundred years effect her operation, and so long an enjoyment of life is not granted us, nor we permitted to live beyond the elephant, or to the year of Plato, as they call it; the philosopher allows a greater degree to the fire, that he may in a shorter time emulate nature as his guide. Wherefore you with good reason will say that he excels in a particular happiness of disposition, who can show you the fire agreeable to, or of, nature.

The philosophers call their natural fire a bath, or their sun, or horse dung; which some make with wood, or any other matter; but we with coals, especially in a furnace fitted for this purpose. The stone is also to be made in a threefold earthen vessel, that there may a slower fire be had, very much like, I say, to the heat of a hen, while she sits on her eggs. And with that heat the dragon, that is the earth of gold, mortifies himself, when he gives elements and spirits out of himself. On the contrary he revives himself, when he hath received the spirits again unto himself. Wherefore he is compared to Jesus Christ, who voluntarily offered himself to death for us, and afterward by his own power, by the glory of his resurrection, restored himself to life never anymore to die. We also say in this place that the dragon spews out of himself all obscurity and venom, and that he afterward imbibes it and is whitened. And because we have said above that heaven ought to be joined with earth, there arises this question: whether heaven ought to descend to the earth, or the earth ought to ascend up to heaven? It is most certain that the earth cannot ascend, unless heaven first descends, but the earth is said to be sublimed up to heaven, when being dissolved in its own spirit, it is at length made one thing with it. I will satisfy you with this similitude: the son of God descending into the virgin, and there flesh, a formed man is born, who when he had for our salvation shown us the way of truth, having suffered and died for us, after the resurrection returns into the heavens. Where earth, that is, humanity, was exalted above all the circles of the world, and placed in the intellectual heaven of the most holy trinity. In the like manner when I die, my soul assisted by the grace and merits of Christ returns unto the vital fountain, from whence it has descended. The body returns unto the earth, which being at length purified in the last judgment of the world, the soul coming down from heaven, leads away with itself to glory. But because it is requisite that the soul should ascend to heaven, another doubt offers itself: that is whether the spirit ought to pass with the soul to heaven, or whether both ought to remain beneath heaven? We have said that the spirit is in this world the bond of which it retains the soul; but when the stone shall have arrived at the first whiteness, there will be another world far more excellent than the former, where the spirit shall remain in the middle, the soul in heaven, and the body in the bottom. Understand the earth to be the heaven of the soul, contrariwise, the soul to be the heaven of the body. And because the spirit has enfeebled the body in solution, they both do penance, and the soul is purged by the spirit, and likewise is the body. Only the soul cleansed from feces ascends up into the heaven, and the spirit goes away with its grimes. If so be that that spirit should stay with the soul and the body, there would be a perpetual corruption there, nor would there be made a right agreement and equality of the elements. This spirit you may fitly liken in some things to an angel who uses to descend with a human soul (when it is infused into the middle point of the heart, and from thence into all parts of the little body.)

We make also the body, soul and spirit speak by the way of dialog, the spirit saying to the soul: "I will lead you to eternal death, to hell and to the dark house." To whom the soul replies: "Spirit of my life; why do you not bring me back again into the bosom from whence by flattery you took me out? I thought myself bound to you by kindred, I truly am your friend, and will bring you to eternal glory."

But the body thinks that by reviving it, he makes it glorious. To whom the spirit says: "I will truly do it, but miserable I, I am forced to be gone when I shall have placed you above all precious stones, and made you blessed. Wherefore I beseech you when you shall have arrived at the throne of the kingdom, to be sometimes mindful of me." To which the body at length gave innumerable thanks, that he had given it a most excellent being, by which he beheld God as in a looking glass, and promised to remember him; and congratulates on the chiefest parts or share in the throne of the kingdom.

Chapter XV

Explains this Proposition: In the shade of the sun is the heat of the moon; and in the heat of the moon is the cold of the sun. Likewise how it is known in the moon, the sun ought to shine. What the shade of the sun and the moon is, and that it is necessary that the sun and the moon and likewise heaven and earth be joined, and makes mention of the citrine Aurora.

We said in the foregoing chapter, that Sol and Lune ought to be joined. We believe you know what Sol is, lastly what Phoebe herself is. Cynthia, that is, Luna opens Phoebus, Sol. Phoebus shuts and coagulates his sister, that is Luna. In the very marriage of Sol and Lune understand this proportion. In the shade of Sol, is the heat of the moon. And in the heat of the moon is the cold of Sol. For when the humidity of Luna has received heat and light from Sol, Sol is said to enter into Luna, at whose entrance Luna revives, increases and begins to grow warm, but Sol to grow cold and moist; because he hath received water to himself and hath lost heat and dryness, whereby losing his share of light, he becomes dark. But when Luna shall go into Sol, Sol himself begins to revive, and Luna bereft of brightness grows thin and is obscured. From whence I assert that the shade of Sol is the coldness and moisture of Luna, but that the shade is the day of Luna. Take the shade therefore from Sol, and his whole light is everywhere dispersed. Yet think not that Luna can take light from the sun in one little space of an hour, but the body is dissolved by little and little. In the beginning when Phoebe is joined to Sol, she is set on fire by him, who being kindled is seen to shine by degrees before midnight; but when she has filled up her whole orb, she uses it to enlighten all the night. Who decreasing again and growing dim for want of light, the heat of

36

Phoebus begins to be vigorous. Where you will plainly know in
Luna when Sol ought to shine, if carrying with you the meaning
of my writings, you run it over inwardly in your mind; though it
may also be understood by other industry. When Luna, that is,
the white stone shall begin to grow citrine and red, it is a token
of Sol shining. The beginning of redness is Aurora. Who would
not call Aurora citrine? Tithonia, that is, Aurora seems to be
bound to this common office to redden the air, and with the first
light to show the rapid journey of Phaeton, that is, of Sol. Where
at length yellow Eous pours out the quick sighted light from the
eastern climate, which seems to be the soul. But that, as it is
argued above, it is necessary that Sol go into Luna, then Luna
into Sol, we discover two intermediate impediments in heaven,
Venus and Mercury, which being taken away there will be a
wonderful copulation of them, which being done, Luna will no
more lose her light, but shine with luster of her own. And Sol, in
a like manner: and the last day of the former world will come,
after which there follows another world, and another life, where
there will be either a perpetual day with those above, or a
perpetual shade with those below: And fire will descend from
heaven and shall again ascend up to the golden heaven, that is,
shall tinge the imperfect.

Chapter XVI

**Of the Augmentation itself of the Stone, both of the ancients
and the modern Philosophers: and it is concluded that there
is but one day and one night. Again seven days from the
seven lords of the world.**

It now pleases me, son of wisdom, to bring that physical
pinnacle into the happy work. Then move the oars, spread the
sails abroad, give a swift and prosperous wind, the safe haven is
to be looked for. After our stone is made white, we call it our

begotten son: though now a child it is a perfect man, consisting of a body and soul; yet it is not able to get another progeny, unless it be first bred up with a nourishment of its own nature, until it arrives at an age mature for generation. We have received from these ancient philosophers, who operated in nature only, that their living water was divided into two parts. Who when they had with one part of the water attained to the fixed whiteness, they rubified it with the other part of the water which was reserved, or perhaps with fire alone. Others in the red stone, because it hath ascended to the highest degree, and cannot be increased by itself, have begun again those works, which they accomplished before, dissolving that redness with the other part of the water, which they had reserved, they again reduced it into the first essence, as I may say. And they worked almost in all things as from the beginning, but truly with a greater industry both of the fire and of the labors: and I believe this repetition to be the truer and the greater augmentation.

Wherefore also the first philosophers used a longer time in finishing the stone. Which their successors and posterity used to end in the course of a year, so that they augmented the white stone (by which they would tinge into silver) with a lunar sperm throughout the whole, or by adding to it other spirits, namely white ones drawn out of tin, and lead by sublimation. Moreover they rubified the white stone with the solar sperm, or other reddish spirits out of iron and copper. And this you may judge was done not amiss, since those inferior bodies have much tincture in them. If so be you should take what is the more perfect out of those bodies and should add it to the more perfect body, what doubt is there that the whole would be made perfect? And such like inferior bodies are called spirits when we say: "Dissolve the body, that is the stone already made, and join the spirits." They are also called children when we say: "Children play with the stone, when they make it greater in weight and virtue." Whence also we in other works know the urine of children of four years old to be the water of the four inferior bodies; which since it is called the *aqua fortis* of the philosophers, is said to dissolve gold, out of which things we do not deny but that a certain stone is made.

The mineral stone we distinguish in three ways. The stone of the philosophers is made out of gold alone and nature alone; and that is the more sublime; which is by the philosophers reported to cure all sicknesses. The second is the simple stone, when the root only, and the sulfur of gold or silver is in the end augmented by the spirits of the inferior bodies. Where these weights set down in the lesser Turba are discussed- One to three, or two to seven, wanting only a golden or a silver sulfur.

The three red spirits are reduced to the golden, the three white ones to the silver sulfur. Now there are two sulfurs and seven spirits out of which the number nine proceeds and is made up, concerning which most men have even unto this day, made foolish comments. We say that the sulfurs of all the metals with their spirits make up the third stone. It is by the most prudent in philosophy thus determined that the stone can tinge innumerable parts. That every spirit is able to be multiplied, but not any body. And since our stone is made extremely volatile, and as I may say, spiritual and all fiery, and nourished in the fire by a long decoction, and very often repeated by very many solutions and by coagulation, why may you not believe that that stone can tinge innumerable parts? If you with judgment do inwardly apprehend the way of nature and her admirable properties. The more often you shall have dissolved it into the white Sol, and again coagulated, the more it will tinge. Also the more wives a man shall have taken, the greater issue he will have.

And a certain philosopher says this: If you shall have given it tincture, it will tinge as you would have it. Which may also be seen in corn and seed, since out of one little grain many are produced, out of which often repeated, there uses to arise at length a rich crop. Nor will this be a lesser argument, if to the sun and moon first conjoined you add their children; that is, the inferior planets, and the planets are the lords of the world, who govern all this mighty mass. What should hinder it, but that the stone composed of all ye metallic things may by tinging the whole world. The same is also manifest concerning the stone out of Gold only, because Sol is the Lord of the other planets, and the rest of the planets take from him a golden luster. From whence it may be concluded that there is but one day and one night in the whole age of the world. Again seven days from the seven planets, and those days one day; because the sun is one: the brightness of the sun, is day, which shining on you, all trouble and calamity does fly away from you.

Chapter XVII

Explains Certain Obscure Proportions laid down in the books of this science.

The Samian Pythagoras when he received scholars into his college to be instructed, is said in the first place to have given them this command; not to publish to the vulgar any of those things which were treated of in their schools. Wherefore he made his hearers be silent for the space of five years, that it might not be lawful for them either to ask their master, or discourse of those things among themselves. Which custom the Pythagoreans following, at length their memory failing, they begun to put into writing those things which they had learned of their master, as well concerning the principles of things, as concerning divine things: so that the secret marrow of those things should be hid in the sacred obligations of numbers. Which that Plato also did (who by doubtful similitudes and mathematical figures hid his precepts is shown by his epistle which he writ to Dionysus concerning the nature of the first being.) We must write, says he, by ambiguities and enigmas, that if the book happen to be cast away by sea or by land, he who should read might not understand it. This I also judge gave occasion to the poets to make their fables, whereby, least things sublime should pass away to the unworthy mob, they laid up the sweetest food of philosophy under the essential bark of little fables. We read that the Egyptians to preserve their determinations, in their holy places, hid them in letters difficult to be known, that is in certain figures of animals, as being the print or sign of nature. If I well remember there was the effigy of a vulture. A dragon drawn into a circle, and biting his own tail, made out the image of the running year. Do not some more curious people endeavor to ascribe everything to it's proper character, whereby there might be a more hidden remark of that thing. Thereby it comes to pass that those ancient philosophers were of opinion to deliver this divine art under more obscure words. The cause you'll find in chapter seven.

Wherefore I thought it requisite and worth the while, if I should explain to you, as to a son of philosophy, some obscure propositions, by which you may easily canvas others which occur. The philosophers say that their stone is found everywhere, in the mountains and in caves. From that proposition evilly understood, I am persuaded that all the errors were derived down to posterity, who works in blood, eggs, hair, and other vain and foreign things. Do you understand it thus? As the celestial sun itself, by its rays is everywhere in this greater world: so this terrestrial Sol, that is gold, is everywhere in the whole glass, that is, in the lesser world: in the mountains, that is, in the head of the glass and in heaven: and in the caverns, that is the bottom of the glass and in the earth. They say the stone is bred in two mountains: in heaven the mountain and in the earth, another mountain, understand it in the glass. Furthermore they affirm their stone to be in all things: that is, in all metals, which are their things. The stone also is in everything, that is, nature is in everything. And because nature has in itself all names, and nature is all the world, therefore the stone has many names and is said to be in everything: although one is nearer than another: since the philosophers demand the generative nature alone of metals. Whence they say that the rich; that is, the perfect bodies, that is the gold and silver, have that nature, as well as the poor, that is, the imperfect metals. Yet the nature of gold or of silver is the more perfect, and the more permanent in the fire, than the rest of the metals. The philosophers also seek a fixed and a permanent thing, which may govern all the world, namely, Sol and Lune. From whence they anciently call the sun the lord of the world: in whom there is life to heal all things, who by his motion makes day and night, and illuminates the whole world with his brightness.

Wherefore Sol says, I am the stone, or, in me is the stone. The philosophers also say: That the work of the stone is the work of a woman, and the play of children. The woman is sometimes the earth, sometimes the mercury, which seems to perfect the whole work. The children play with the stone, that is, the three elements with the earth, or the inferior bodies play with the golden stone, when they augment it in the end. Likewise, children play with the stone and cast it away, that is, ignorant and unskillful folks cast away the earth itself in the bottom, when they have made sublimation. Some philosophers have compared the work of the stone to the creation of the world. Likewise to the generation of man, and to his naturalness.

A Book of Alchemy

But the more modern philosophers have hidden this
knowledge not only in new words, but also in painted images. I
have seen painted by a most goodly pencil, a naked virgin, of a
tender age, with hair like ivory, black eyes, white and red cheeks,
whose breasts were milky, very smooth and round. And that
virgin was in all the beauty of the body so excellent and so
handsomely adorned with all the endowments of nature, that she
might be thought most worthy of a royal bed, and with whom
also all philosophers, both the ancient and the modern might be
deeply in love. Such as the poets use to describe Venus, or Juno,
or any other beautiful maid or damsel. But that nymph had in her
hands hung down, two mighty burning torches, and under her
right foot there was a golden stone out of whose bosom a certain
golden fountain ran forth into many little veins. Under her left
foot there was a silver stone, vomiting out of itself a silver flame.
On the right hand Titan himself was painted, with his rays
sparkling all round about. On the left were described the horns of
Phoebe: there flew about certain birds partly upward into the air,
partly downward to the earth. At the Virgin's back you see there
has grown up a tree replenished with diverse apples and flowers,
which you would take to be the Tree of Life planted in the
Garden of Paradise, if you did taste its flavor and liveliness.
Hermes is described in his philosophical miter, evidently the
chief of all the philosophers, sitting in a chair, holding two tables
on his knees; in one whereof there were delineated both the
globe of the sun and the horned moon; under whom there were
two birds drawn into a circle mutually swallowing one another;
whereof one, the uppermost was painted with wings, the other
without. In the other table there were painted three changeably-
colored circles, in the middle of which was the image of the
moon, to whom two suns, one of them darted out one ray, the
other two: and nine eagles flew about Hermes' chair, having in
their feet, bent bows, from which feathered arrows were shot
down unto the Earth. Has not one Ulmannus a Friar Minorite of
the order of Saint Francis with a most admirable dexterity woven

out our science in his own country's language and mother tongue? And by Christ's passion proved it most true? Where there is seen that double shaped Image, partly male, partly female, that hermaphroditic being, carrying in its hand a scepter of imperial majesty: and many other things of that kind are seen in the books of the philosophers.

Chapter XVIII

Shows that the Stone can Cure all Sicknesses: since all Nature is in the sun, and the sun in Nature, and especially in the stone.

But that the stone can cure all sickness, of these all the books of the philosophers are full. Yet I will according to my best ability study to demonstrate it. All nature is in the sun, and the sun in nature. Therefore we may catch his spirit in all things, but especially in gold. And when nature is sick, that stone cures nature. In propagating gold Heaven has taken the greatest pains; likewise the sun itself, and Jupiter. The sun has put all his endowments into it, by reason of its fiery virtue and brightness. But Jupiter whom the physicians call the patron of life, has infused into it temperance and an equality of the elements. By these gifts Gold is made so incorruptible, that no fire can by destroying act upon its substance and virtue. To these are added the solution of gold, the purification of its nature, and a long nourishment in fire, by which it has obtained a wonderful and almost divine operation. If so be you should take in victuals or in drink the weight of a grain of mustard seed, it by its celestial vigor would preserve in an equality the oil and fire of life, and would temper and tie together the elements of your body in peace. Which being tempered, the soul would abide with the elements and man would remain always sound, until that end which the omnipotent God has ordained by reason of the disobedience of our first parent. There was in Christ's body so great an affinity, and so great a binding together of the elements, because he was liable to sin, as also by reason of the wonderful union of the divine essence, that he had never died naturally, had he not for the sake of redeeming, man willingly desired death.

Render him perpetual thanks for creating you, for redeeming you from the infernal regions with his precious blood, and for bestowing on you so great a gift as this. Whereby you may lead a long life and have health in happiness, for which chiefly our stone is to be sought after. I say nothing of the plenty of riches, with which a man by this art most fully and copiously abounds. If having the *Aurum potable* or the golden liquor, you shall dissolve that stone in *aqua vitae* drawn out of malmsey wine, or some other falernum, that is, rich wine.

Chapter XIX

Repeats the Philosophical Praxis, where the divine skill of the stone is often times all of it set down in short sentences.

Mix the masculine prince with mercury in a twelfth proportion in respect of the prince. Put it to a slow fire and continue it, until the mercury dissolving the bodies there appear aloft. A Venus swimming, which extracts until nothing of the body remains in the bottom, and you have the first part of the physical work. The second part of the work is sulfur, put that in a glass without water, and by distilling the water of the body, in which there is the soul of Lune. Join this water with the sulfur, and permit many times, one to arise sometimes with the other, sometimes to descend as well: until Venus shall have conceived her water, which is done in a most white color, and you have the elixir to the white. The third part of the work is: You shall make citrine with a strong fire, the most white, earth which you have obtained: afterward you shall rubify it by the force of fire, and it is the elixir to the red.

Of another way of working: Still I have a mind to contain in short, and with admirable art that divine knowledge. Dissolve the body, take the sulfur, cleanse it, sublime the spirit, join the spirit with the sulfur, and you will have the physical art. In every perfect alchemical work, though never so small, it is necessary to have the spirit and sulfur of gold. The spirit tinges with a golden color. The sulfur gives the weight of gold, and coagulates.

If it wanted either, the work would be nothing. Then say and speak the greatest truth, that all the secret of nature lies hid in the Venus of the physical gold. Wherefore it is wont to be called the coagulation; when it is said: take that coagulate from the body, and you have a magistery, than which there is not a greater in nature. Likewise cleanse the coagulate, and destroy the impediment, and you will tinge. But because a dirty cloth, not compared to sulfur, cannot be washed without water. To wash is to dissolve, to dissolve is to purify, the water is mercury, it is the key. It alone does open the body, and whitens the sulfur, which being whitened, it recedes with uncleanliness. I would say you were admirably learned if you should be able to remove it, the uncleanliness, it is the impediment and eternal death. Wherefore it shall not go to heaven, as above in chapter fourteen I have plainly demonstrated. And I say unto you by God the creator of heaven, it is one of the greatest secrets. Furthermore, the very knowledge of the stone is no other thing than the purification of the earth, or of nature. The earth cannot be cleared from feces and purged, unless through the middle or center it shall have received the water unto itself. And this comprehends the whole art in short, if you have understood nature. You may of yourself by divine grace discover many things like unto these. Praise God for all ages of ages.

Here ends my consideration.

Hereby he affirms himself to be an Adept. But there may be many reasons unknown to us: I question not but the Inquisition was the reason of his suppressing his name.

Chapter XX

Lays down the Questions put by Illardus the Necromancer to the devil, concerning the stone of the Philosophers.

A certain Necromancer, Illardus by name in the province of Catalonia put these questions to the devil.

Whether the stone of the Philosophers can be made, to convert the imperfect metals into Gold and Silver, fire being the judge?

All metals are essentially in gold, with their earths in a manifold color. Out of its earth with its own essence the stone is made, which by its nature takes all uncleanliness away, and being projected on the imperfect metals, fixes them forever.

What and what kind of a essence is that?

It is a soul, a middle nature, which permits one form to be converted into another.

In what manner does the soul, the middle nature, act?

Neither angels, nor men in any wise inwardly behold or comprehend it by their acutest understandings. Because this is proper to God who reserved this to his own majesty.

Can man make the stone?

Whatever God has created, having a property, it is possible for man to act upon it, but it is very hard to make the stone, yet it may be made.

The soul, the middle nature has it a body?

The color of gold is the body of the soul, the middle nature.

By what way can the color be separated from Gold?

The soul, the middle nature, with its heat and moisture does divide and conjoin both together.

The color of Gold, is it white, or black or of what sort?

It is white to man's sight, but in spirit it is blue.

In what manner, and out of what is color made?

Nature makes it out of a pure earth and pure water.

Is there a color in all metals?

Not only in metals, but also in all the elements there is a hidden color.

Of what virtue, or power is the stone?

The stone can purify all the imperfect metallic bodies from all leprosy, so that they shall be perpetual even to the last judgment. It cures human bodies of all sickness, until a natural death.

Of what sort, and what thing is the soul of a human body?

It is the living fire of a heavenly life, and hath in itself, the soul, the middle nature. By the soul, the middle nature, God is called the creator of all things which are in the world.

Had Virgil the stone?

Not only did he have it, but many philosophers had it, and have written in diverse ways about it under obscure names and may operations.

How and why is it called the stone?

I tell you that the stone is its name, and there is no permission given me to let you know more.

In what time can the stone be brought to an end?

Twelve months are necessary from the first day of the beginning. In thirty days an earth is generated out of lead, or the nature of the earth makes lead grow. In one hundred days *argent vive* grows in water. In sixty days completed there grew a vapor out of tin completed. In the other days of the year, fire grows from gold. In the moment of the year ending, the soul, the middle nature, descends from heaven into this earth, and mortifies the superior and inferior powers. The image of a manifold victory to consume the war in the heart of the belly of them, even to the perpetual judgment of fire. I will tell you no more.

THE END

Made in the USA
Las Vegas, NV
13 June 2022

50195902R00030